The Giver

by
Lois Lowry

Student Packet

Written by:
Phyllis A. Green

Contains masters for:

- 1 Initiating Activity
- 1 Study Guide—8 pages
- 4 Vocabulary Activities
- 1 Writing/Journal
- 2 Character Analyses
- 1 Expression
- 1 Art
- 1 Drama
- 2 Analyses
- 1 Number Teasers
- 1 Visualization
- 1 Summarizing
- 1 Comparison/Contrast
- 1 Comprehension Quiz – After Chapter 6
- 1 Comprehension Quiz – After Chapter 12
- 1 Comprehension Quiz – After Chapter 18
- 1 Final Examination
- 1 Essay Protocol/Rubric

PLUS Detailed Answer Key

Note
The Laurel Leaf Newberry paperback edition was used to prepare this guide. Page references may vary if other editions are used.

ISBN 1-56137-717-1

© 1998 Novel Units, Inc. All rights reserved. Printed in the United States of America. Limited reproduction permission: The publisher grants permission to individual teachers who have purchased this book, or for whom it has been purchased, to reproduce the blackline masters as needed for use with their own students. Reproduction for an entire school or school district or for commercial use is prohibited.

To order, contact your local school supply store, or—

Novel Units, Inc.
P.O. Box 791610
San Antonio, TX 78279

Name_____

The Giver
Activity #1: Initiating Activity –
Use Before Reading

Dear Reader,

The Giver is an award-winning book. The author, Lois Lowry, uses language to paint vivid pictures. Her choice of words is strong and purposeful. Here are some facts about this book:

1. It is serious. It has a strong purpose and message.
2. It is science fiction. The plot is beyond earthly reality.
3. The book's society favors a controlled, very predictable, efficient existence over a creative, unpredictable way of life.

Ponder these ideas and then free write your own ideas about the book's theme, as well as what you expect from such a book.

Enjoy!

_____

_____

_____

_____

_____

_____

_____

_____

_____

_____

_____

Name_____

The Giver
Study Guide – Page 1

Study Guide

Directions: These questions are provided to assist the reader to understand the literal details of the book. A few opinion questions are also included. Your teacher will direct you in responding to the questions.

1. Write out short answers.

2. Be prepared to answer orally.

3. Make notes to enable small group discussion.

4. Preview the questions prior to reading a section.

Chapter 1, Pages 1-10

1. What is the point-of-view in the story? _____
_____
_____
_____

2. What do you learn about each of Jonas's family members from his/her sharing of feelings after dinner? _____
_____
_____
_____

3. What kind of punishments are used in the book's society? _____
_____
_____
_____

4. What is the setting (time and place) of the book? _____
_____
_____

Name_____

The Giver
Study Guide – Page 2

Chapter 2, Pages 11-19
1. What are some of the structural guidelines in the book's society?

2. What does it mean to be "politically correct" in the book's society?

3. What is especially momentous about the Ceremony of Twelve?

Chapter 3, Pages 20-25
1. What is the attitude toward mirrors in the book? What does it tell you about the society in general?

2. How do the book folks feel about mothering? How is it different from what you've known and experienced?

3. Why does Jonas keep the apple to investigate?

Chapter 4, Pages 26-33
1. What have the volunteer hours done for Benjamin and Fiona? What about Jonas?

2. Why does Jonas especially like the feeling of safety in the House of the Old?

Name_____

The Giver
Study Guide – Page 3

3. What have you learned so far about *releasing*?

4. What is the reaction when a new idea is suggested and referred to committee?

Chapter 5, Pages 34-39
1. Explain the society's rule about stirrings.

2. Why are the rules printed all in caps?

Chapter 6, Pages 40-49
1. What is the mood on the day of the Ceremonies?

2. What kind of power does the Committee of Elders have?

Chapter 7, Pages 50-58
1. How does Jonas feel as his Ceremony of Twelve starts? when number twenty is announced?

Name_____ *The Giver*
Study Guide – Page 4

2. What do you think Jonas has done wrong?
_____
_____
_____

3. How are the assignments decided? Are they appropriate?
_____
_____
_____
_____

Chapter 8, Pages 59-64
1. Why is Jonas' assignment "a selection"?
_____
_____
_____

2. What is the "capacity to see beyond"?
_____
_____
_____

3. Why does the community cheer for Jonas?
_____
_____
_____

Chapter 9, Pages 65-71
1. How have things changed after the Ceremony of Twelve?
_____
_____
_____

2. What is puzzling for Jonas about his instructions for Receiver training?
_____
_____
_____

Name_____

The Giver
Study Guide – Page 5

3. How would you feel if you'd received the instructions Jonas did?

Chapter 10, Pages 72-79
1. What will Jonas' training entail?

2. What is the first memory transmitted to Jonas?

3. How does the author let you know that Jonas' training will be astonishing for him?

Chapter 11, Pages 80-87
1. How does it feel for Jonas as he receives memories?

2. Why doesn't the book's world have snow, sleds and hills except in the Receiver's memory?

3. How does Jonas react to sunburn?

Chapter 12, Pages 88-96
1. How is "seeing beyond" developing for Jonas?

Name_____

The Giver
Study Guide – Page 6

2. What is the difference between one-generation memories and the memory Jonas is receiving?

Chapter 13, Pages 97-107
1. Why does Jonas begin to feel unfairness in his world?

2. Why doesn't Jonas' family understand his training?

3. Why does Jonas decide to keep secret how he calms Gabriel?

Chapter 15, Pages 118-120
1. How does Jonas help The Giver in Chapter 15?

2. What is the memory that so tortures The Giver?

Chapter 16, Pages 121-129
1. Why doesn't Jonas want to return to The Giver at the start of the chapter?

2. Why does Jonas need to learn the joy of being an individual—special, unique, and proud?

© Novel Units, Inc.　　　　　　　　　　　　　　　　　　　　　　　All rights reserved

Name_____

The Giver
Study Guide – Page 7

3. How do Jonas and his parents differ in their understanding of love?

Chapter 17, Pages 130-138
1. How are Jonas' feelings different from his family's feelings?

2. What has Jonas lost as the Receiver of Memories?

Chapter 18, Pages 139-145
1. Who was Rosemary and what happened to her?

2. Why is the Receiver's job so vital to the book's community?

Chapter 19, Pages 146-151
1. Why does the author use italics on page 147? How is Jonas' answer significant and important to the plot and his own development?

2. What does Jonas learn about release? How does it make him feel?

Name_____

The Giver
Study Guide – Page 8

Chapter 20, Pages 152-162
1. Why does The Giver tell Jonas that the characters in the book know nothing?

2. Why is the Receiver's job lonely?

3. How do Jonas and The Giver plan to change the society in the book?

Chapter 21, Pages 163-170
1. Why doesn't the plan for Jonas' escape work out?

Chapter 22, Pages 171-174
1. What new things and images and feelings do Jonas and Gabe experience in Chapter 22?

2. How does Jonas come no longer to care about himself?

Chapter 23, Pages 175-180
1. How are these details significant in Chapter 23: weather, snow, sled, music?

Name_____

The Giver
Activity #2: Identified Vocabulary Words –
Distribute Before Reading

Vocabulary

Directions: Here are some vocabulary challenges for you, identified chapter-by-chapter. You need to know these words to read the book with understanding. You may want to review the words before reading each chapter to alert yourself. Figure out what you can from context. Use dictionaries if need be. Enjoy and read on.

Chapter 1
rasping
palpable
distraught
distracted
wheedle
nurturer
disposition
transgression
apprehensive

Chapter 2
aptitude

Chapter 3
chastise
rarity
petulantly
bewilderment
nondescript

Chapter 4
gravitating
chortled

Chapter 5
infraction
dosage

Chapter 6
interdependence
indulgently
exuberant
chastisement
transgressions
buoyancy

Chapter 7
exasperated
retroactive
acquisition

Chapter 8
crescendo
humiliation
benign
anguish
meticulously

© Novel Units, Inc.   All rights reserved

Name_____   *The Giver*
Activity #2: Identified Vocabulary Words –
Page 2

Chapter 9	**Chapter 10**	**Chapter 11**	**Chapter 12**
requisitioned excruciating reeled	exhilarating deftly	conveyance	admonition

Chapter 13	**Chapter 14**	**Chapter 15**	**Chapter 16**
mutilated sinuous electrode	skittered acceleration writhing anguish assuage excruciating distended ominous placidly	contorted carnage immobilized	ecstatic obsolete

Chapter 17	**Chapter 18**	**Chapter 19**	**Chapter 20**
permeated exasperation expertise	luminous anguish imploringly		empowered rueful

Chapter 21	**Chapter 22**	**Chapter 23**	
meticulously stealthily frazzled emphatically	exquisite tantalizing	imperceptibly agonizingly trudged lethargy	

Name_____

The Giver
Activity #3: Vocabulary

Vocabulary Cards

Directions: Match your vocabulary activity cards with selected groups of vocabulary words. Then fill in the prompts.

A
_____ and _____ go together because _____
_____
_____
_____.

B
_____ , _____ , and _____ are ten dollar words because_____
_____
_____.

C
I've packed four vocabulary words into this sentence. _____
_____
_____
_____.

D
_____ , _____ ,
_____ , _____ ,
and_____ are special ways to move.

E
Create an analogy with the words
_____is to _____
as
_____is to _____

F
_____and_____ don't go together because _____
_____
_____
_____.

Name_____

The Giver
Activity #4: Vocabulary – Page 1

The Great Prefix and Suffix Search

1. Use these suffixes (-ion, -ment, -ise, -ance) to make nouns. Find examples from the book and examples from your other experiences.

_____   _____   _____

_____   _____   _____

_____   _____   _____

2. These suffixes (-ful, -ous) are used to make adjectives. Locate 6 examples.

_____   _____   _____

_____   _____   _____

3. What do these prefixes mean?

in-	
inter-	
ex-	
trans-	
non-	
dis-	

Name_____

The Giver
Activity #4: Vocabulary – Page 2

4. Start chains for each of the prefixes and suffixes noted above. List as many words as you can.

-ion

-ment

-ise

-ance

-ful

-ous

in-

inter-

ex-

trans-

non-

dis-

Name_____

The Giver
Activity #5: Vocabulary

Vocabulary Bingo

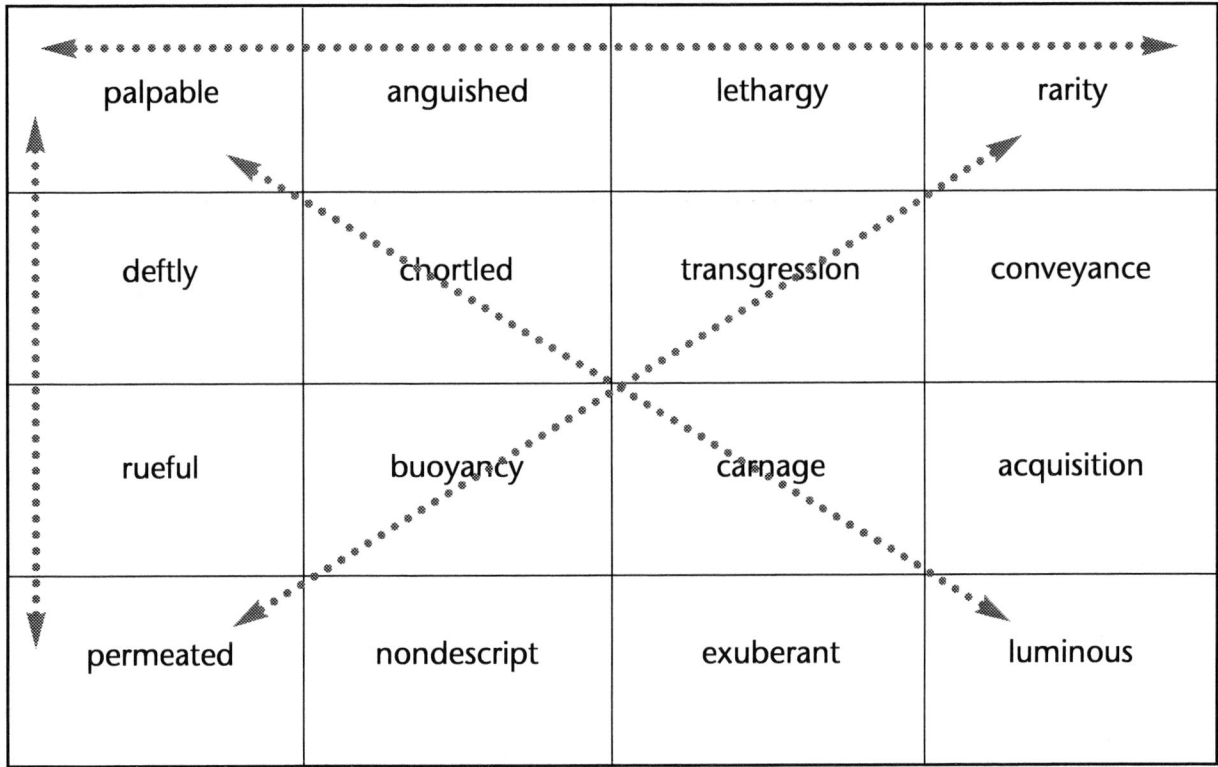

Directions: Working with a small group, write as many sentences as you can. For each sentence, you must include four adjacent words on the Bingo card above. You can use traditional Bingo lines or any other grouping of four adjacent words. Your sentences can be a little silly, but the words should be used properly. Before the group begins, you will need to divide the words among yourselves and find definitions, then share the definitions with the group. Use the back of your paper or a separate sheet for your sentences.

Name_____
The Giver
Activity #6: Writing

Journal Ideas

Directions: Explore some of the ideas in the book with a daily written journal entry. Here are some ideas which you might consider. Feel free to expand on these ideas.

- I disagree with some of the ideas in the book. Specifically,...
- Predictability is something I prize.
- What you prize tells a lot about you.
- What a society values reveals a great deal about the people and their leaders.
- Analyze a rule in the book's society. Explain the plusses and minuses and then recommend or condemn the idea.
- What do colors mean to you?
- What do colors add to the quality of your life?
- My most treasured happy memories are _____.
- How are memories special?
- Science fiction is...
- Why is reading special?
- What are some of your favorite books?
- Why don't the homes and folks in the book have books?
- Is our current society moving in the direction of the society in the book? Why or why not?

© Novel Units, Inc. All rights reserved

Name_____

The Giver
Activity #7: Character Analysis

 Jonas' Emotions

Directions: Choose chapters and specific events from the book for each of these feelings/emotional states that Jonas experiences:

Apprehensive	
Angry	
Frightened	
Happy	
Annoyed	
Intrigued	
Relieved	
Nurturing	

Name_____

The Giver
Activity #8: Expression

Naming

Directions: Match each of Lowry's designations in Column A with a more familiar phraseology from Column B.

A	B
_____ 1. family's dwelling	A. career
_____ 2. learning community	B. mother/father
_____ 3. childcare group	C. stuffed animal
_____ 4. new children	D. garbage collectors
_____ 5. nurturer	E. home
_____ 6. family unit	F. daycare class
_____ 7. assignment	G. babies
_____ 8. citizen-in-training	H. class
_____ 9. comfort object	I. family
_____ 10. food collectors	J. adolescent

What is the impact for you as a reader of Lowry's naming?

_____
_____
_____
_____
_____
_____
_____
_____
_____
_____

© Novel Units, Inc.   All rights reserved

Name_____
The Giver
Activity #9: Art – Page 1

Create a Bit of Art for *The Giver*

Directions: Make sense of the novel and its characters by choosing one of these ideas to represent the themes or people of the book. Explain your creation and choice in a sentence or two.

stationery

baseball card

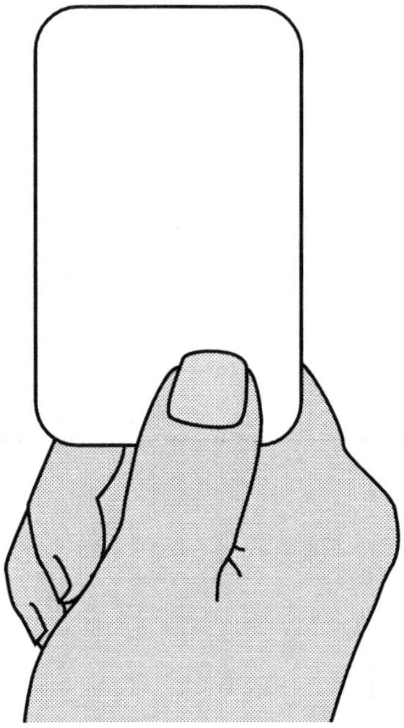

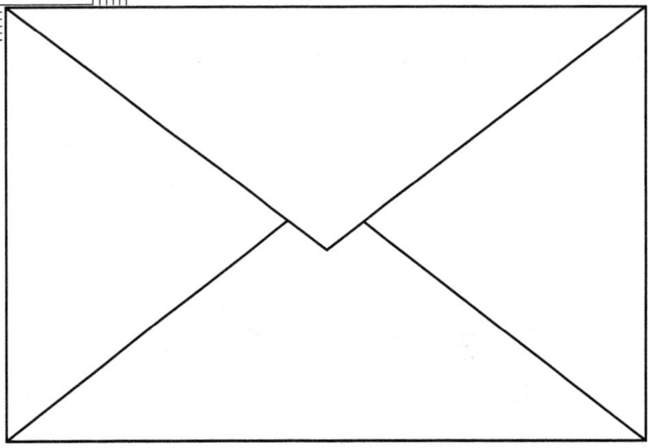

button

© Novel Units, Inc.

Name_____

The Giver
Activity #9: Art– Page 2

postcard

t-shirt

logo

bumper sticker

Name_____

The Giver
Activity #10: Drama

Celebrate *The Giver* Orally

Directions: Make sense of the book's characters and themes in one of these oral ways.

- Hot Seat - Assume the persona of a chosen character. Answer questions of classmates, remaining in character, until they've successfully guessed who you are.

- Prepare a Readers' Theater presentation of a memorable part of the book.

- Read aloud a special part of the book adding your own hand motions.

- Improvisation - Choose a character from Column A and a prompt from Column B. Orally answer the question or provide the item for that particular character.

A Characters	B What to Provide
Giver Jonas Lily - as a grown-up Fiona Gabe - as a baby Gabe - as an adult Lily - as in the book	A recipe Head-to-toe description Favorite music Best book A narrow escape

© Novel Units, Inc. All rights reserved

Name_____

The Giver
Activity #11: Analysis

The Numbers Game

Directions: Explore the pervasiveness* of numbers in the book and in your own life by filling in the jigsaw.

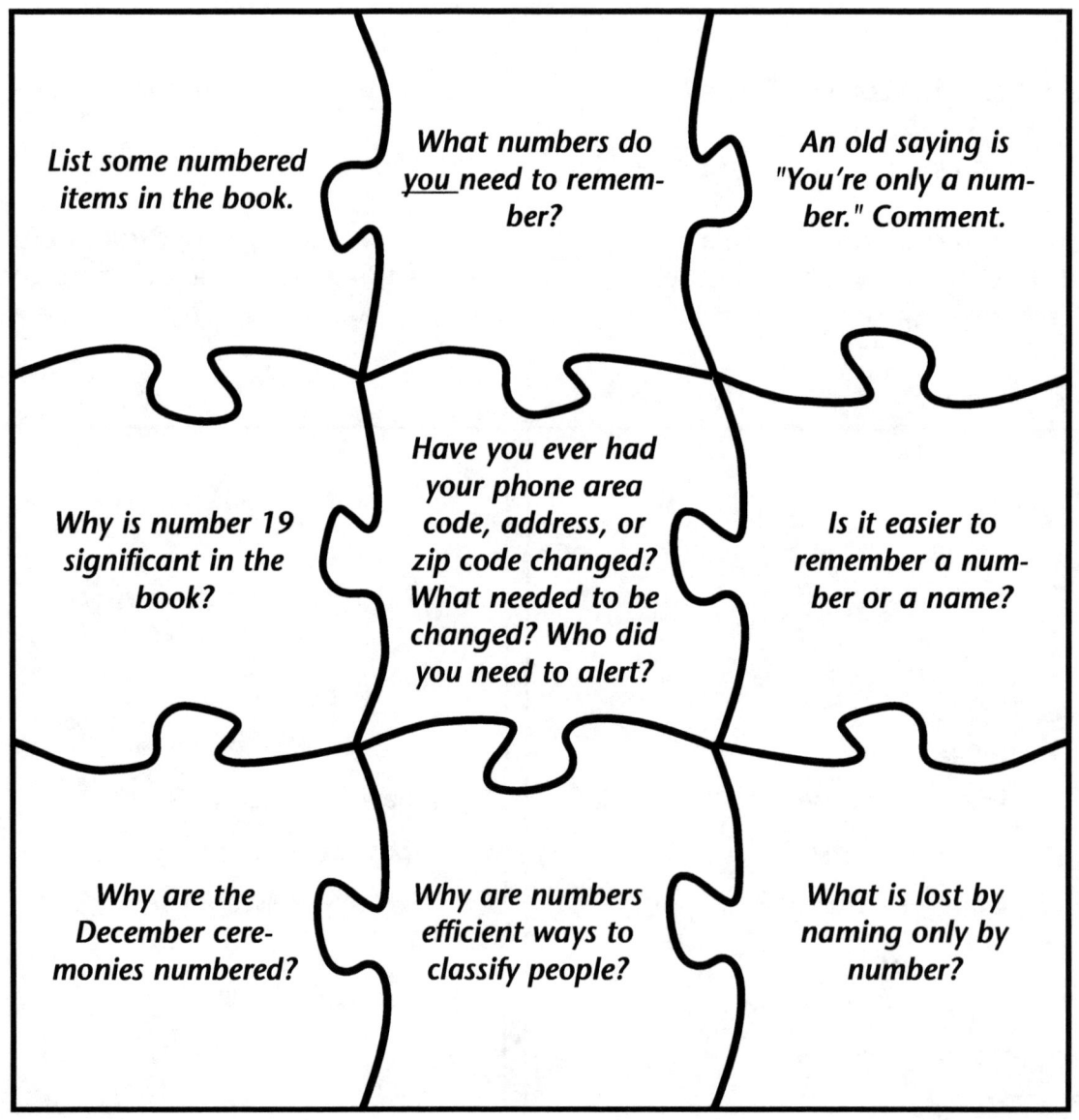

List some numbered items in the book.	What numbers do you need to remember?	An old saying is "You're only a number." Comment.
Why is number 19 significant in the book?	Have you ever had your phone area code, address, or zip code changed? What needed to be changed? Who did you need to alert?	Is it easier to remember a number or a name?
Why are the December ceremonies numbered?	Why are numbers efficient ways to classify people?	What is lost by naming only by number?

* What does pervasiveness mean?

© Novel Units, Inc.   All rights reserved

Name_____

The Giver
Activity #12: Number Teasers

Number Teasers for Fun

Directions: Each of the following phrases uses a number in a common phrase. Try to fill in the words to make the phrase complete

26 L in the A _____

7 D of the W _____

13 in a B D _____

50 S in the U _____

52 C in a D _____

10 Y in a D _____

88 P K _____

24 H in a D _____

9 J in the S C _____

8 S on a S S _____

5 D in a Z C _____

© Novel Units, Inc.   All rights reserved

Name_____

The Giver
Activity #13: Analysis

Comparisons

Directions: Choose one of these pairs to compare.
- the world of the book and your world
- your mother/family and Jonas' mother/family
- choice of occupation in the book and in your world

Use a T-diagram and then transfer to a Venn.

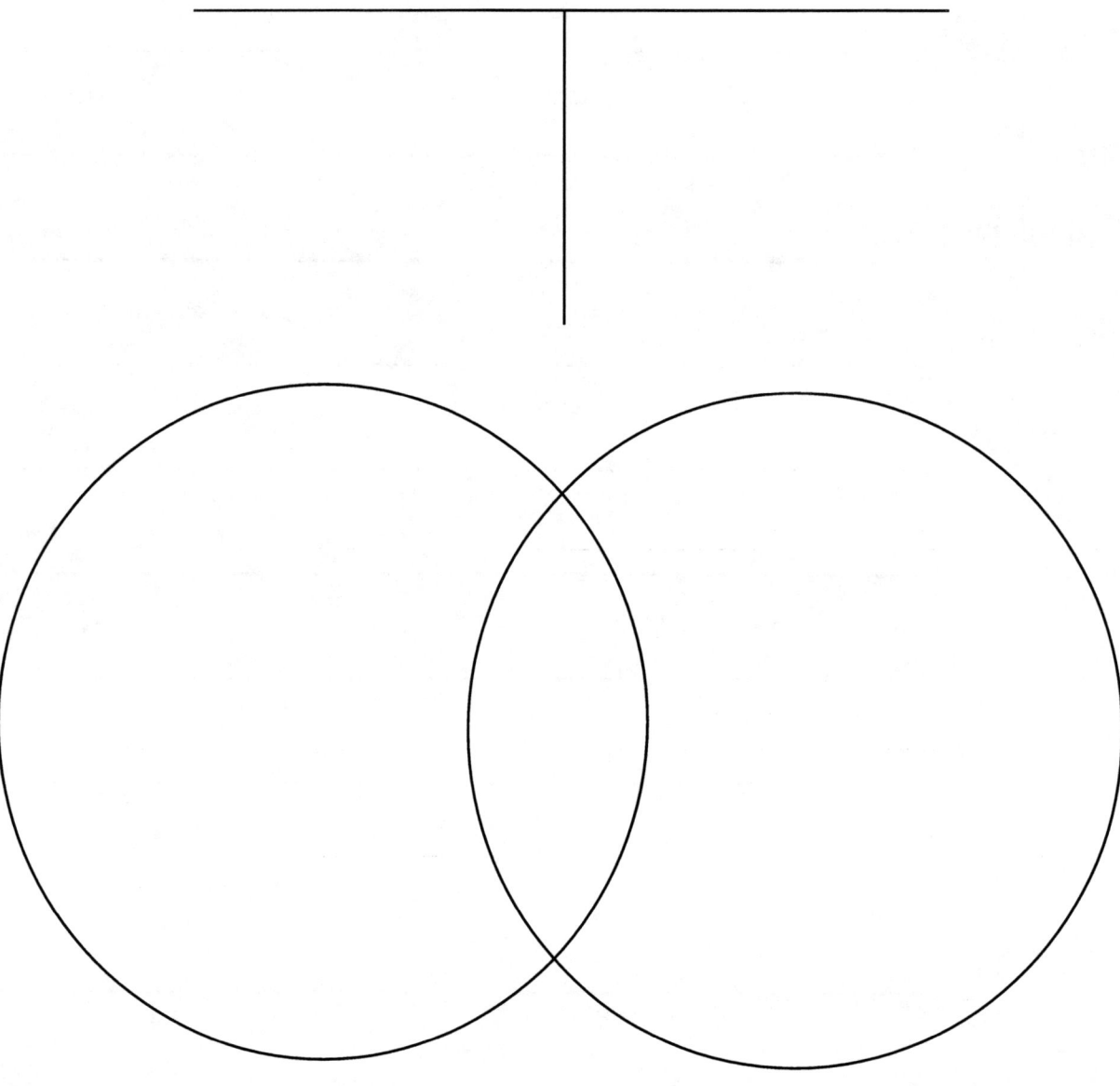

© Novel Units, Inc.

All rights reserved

Name_____

The Giver
Activity #14: Visualization
(After Chapter 12)

Seeing Beyond: Color in the Book

Directions: Choose one of these glimpses from the book to illustrate twice, once as Jonas sees it and then as the rest of the book's people (except The Giver) see it.
- The apple
- Fiona
- The sled ride

Jonas	Everyone Else

© Novel Units, Inc.   All rights reserved

Name_____

The Giver
Activity #15: Character Analysis

Character Analysis

Directions: Complete stars for these four characters from the book. On the points of the stars list what makes that character different or distinctive. On the center of the star, describe one way the character is similar to other characters in the book.

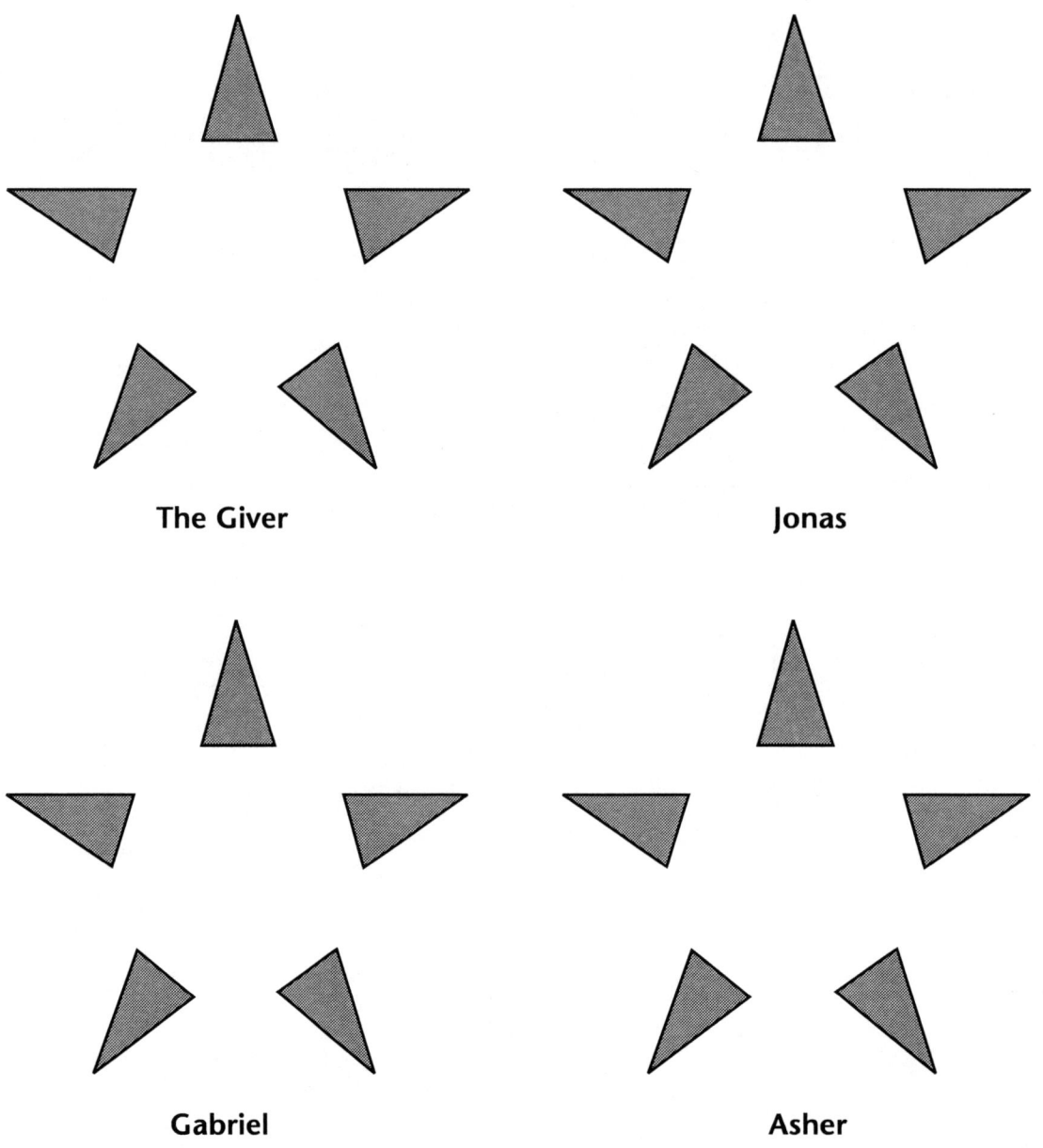

The Giver

Jonas

Gabriel

Asher

© Novel Units, Inc.

All rights reserved

Name_____

The Giver
Activity #16: Summarizing

ABC

Directions: Create an ABC book which reflects the contents of the novel. For example: A is for Asher whose antics and fun make him memorable.

A		**N**	
B		**O**	
C		**P**	
D		**Q**	
E		**R**	
F		**S**	
G		**T**	
H		**U**	
I		**V**	
J		**W**	
K		**X**	
L		**Y**	
M		**Z**	

© Novel Units, Inc. All rights reserved

Name_____

The Giver
Activity #17: Comparison/Contrast

Comparisons

Directions: Fill in the chart to record the setting in the book. Then use the same categories to describe your world.

Category	In the Book	Today in Your World
Transportation		
Government		
Education		
Feelings		
The Scenery		

Name_____

The Giver
Quiz #1
After Reading Chapter 6

Comprehension Check #1

Part I –
Match these numbered details from the book with an appropriate letter.

____ 1. Asher	A. stuffed animal, for example
____ 2. Fiona	B. termed uncertain
____ 3. Lily	C. caused Jonas to be embarrassed and to apologize
____ 4. Jonas	D. careless and fun-loving
____ 5. Gabriel	E. occupation
____ 6. Nurturer	F. father
____ 7. assignment	G. make decisions for the community
____ 8. comfort object	H. teller of the story
____ 9. Committee of Elders	I. released
____ 10. apple	J. in Jonas' dream
	K. jurist
	L. a pacifier
	M. almost an eight

Part II –
Choose one of these words to fill in a word map.

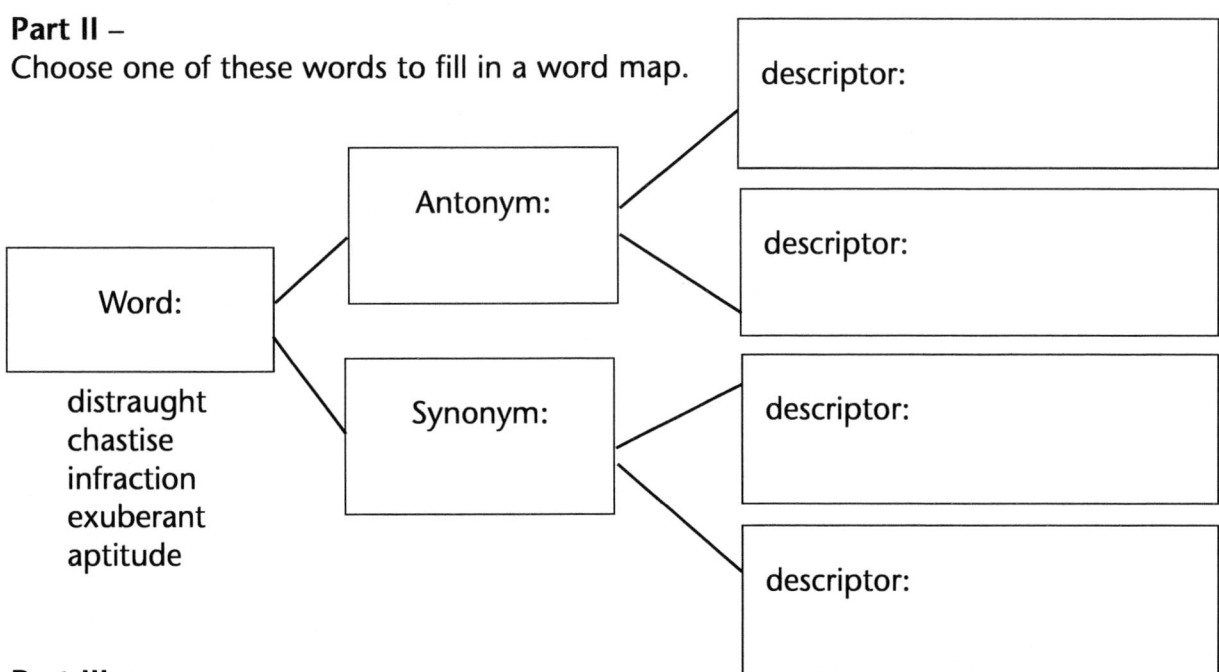

distraught
chastise
infraction
exuberant
aptitude

Part III –
The first six chapters have introduced you to the book's society. In a short paragraph, describe it.

Name_____

The Giver
Quiz #2
After Reading Chapter 12

Comprehension Check #2

Part I –

Draw a pair of pictures–one of the book's world and another of your world. Point out the details you have included.

Part II –

This book is science fiction. Start an attribute web to record ideas about that kind of book.

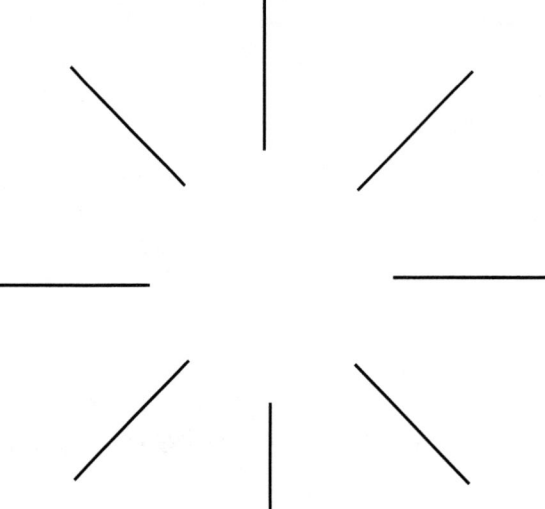

Name_____

The Giver
Quiz #3
After Reading Chapter 18

Comprehension Check #3

Short Answer:
Answer in a short paragraph.

1. How does Jonas change in his year of training as Receiver?

_____
_____
_____
_____

2. What do you know of The Giver? Collect your ideas on this web.

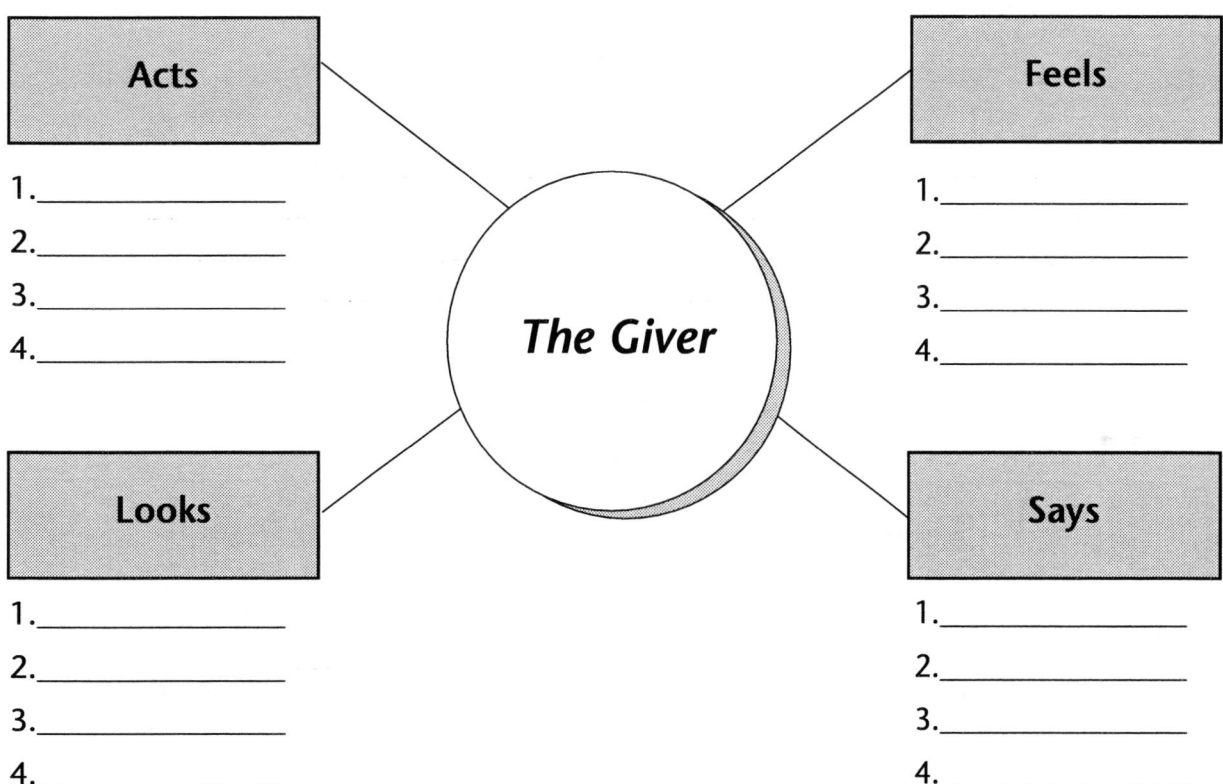

Acts
1._____
2._____
3._____
4._____

Feels
1._____
2._____
3._____
4._____

Looks
1._____
2._____
3._____
4._____

Says
1._____
2._____
3._____
4._____

3. Vocabulary: Choose 3 words to use in sentences.

mutilated	excruciating	skittered
sinuous	anguish	carnage
electrode	ominous	obsolete
ecstatic	expertise	luminous

Name_____

The Giver
Final Examination – Page 1

Final Examination

Part I – Vocabulary matching

Column A	Column B
_____ 1. lethargy	A. caution
_____ 2. tantalizing	B. suffering
_____ 3. rueful	C. favorable
_____ 4. meticulously	D. ability to float
_____ 5. anguish	E. butchery
_____ 6. permeated	F. chuckled
_____ 7. ecstatic	G. skillfully
_____ 8. carnage	H. delighted
_____ 9. sinuous	I. drowsiness
_____ 10. admonition	J. precisely
_____ 11. deftly	K. obvious
_____ 12. benign	L. penetrated
_____ 13. buoyancy	M. mournful
_____ 14. chortled	N. curvy
_____ 15. palpable	O. intriguing

Part II – Recognizing and matching details

Column A	Column B
_____ 1. Red	A. held by the Receiver
_____ 2. Music	B. danger when Jonas escaped
_____ 3. Pain	C. limited in most households
_____ 4. Books	D. Jonas' first evidence of seeing beyond
_____ 5. Rosemary	E. Author
_____ 6. Lowry	F. Killing
_____ 7. Release	G. The Giver's special awareness
_____ 8. Memories	H. Medication
_____ 9. Snow	I. largely eliminated
_____ 10. Relief-of-pain	J. The Giver's daughter

© Novel Units, Inc. All rights reserved

Name_____

The Giver
Final Examination – Page 2

Part III – Collecting ideas
Choose one of these graphics to complete about the characters, actions, or ideas in the book.

A. Trace a typical life in the book's society. Use a timeline or a flow chart.

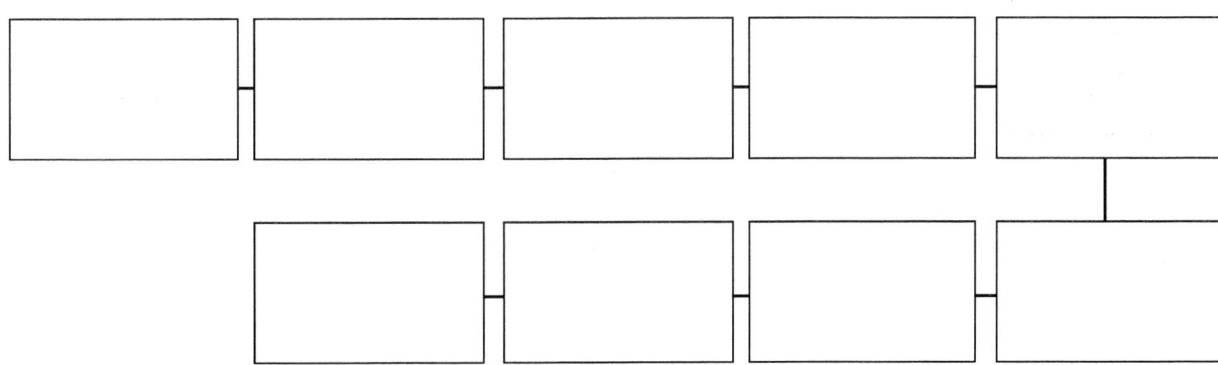

B. Complete a character chart or a character comparison chart.

C. What is Lowry's message in the book? Defend your answer in a short paragraph.

_____
_____
_____
_____
_____

Name_____

The Giver
Final Examination – Page 3

D. Significant ideas in the book: collect ideas on an attribute web.

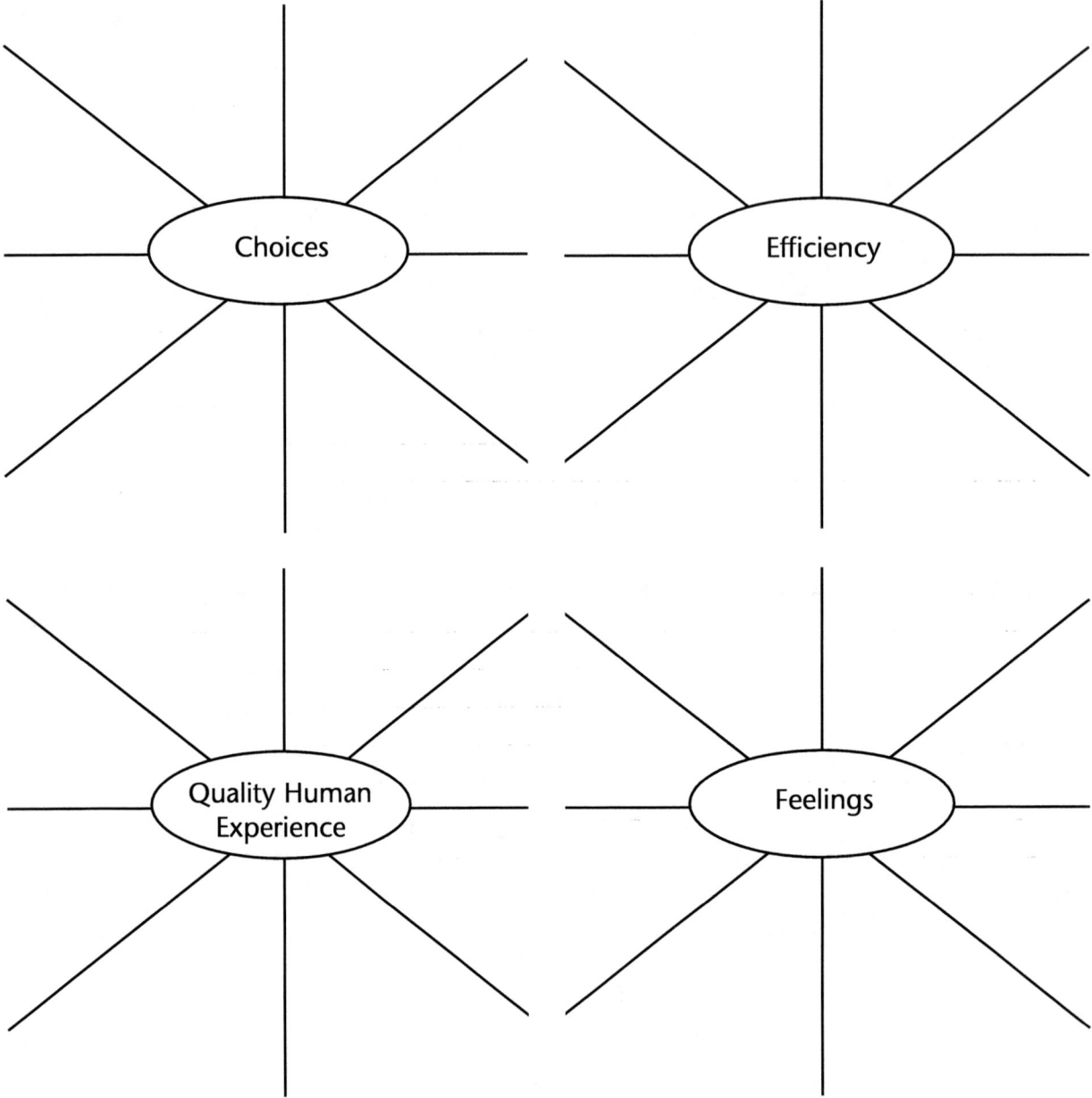

Extra Credit
Look back at your answers in D. Can you figure out any organizing principle?

The Giver

Suggested Answers

Study Guide Questions
Chapter 1
1. (3rd person) Jonas, an eleven-year-old male
2. Lily, Jonas' sister, is a lively seven-year-old who is learning to appreciate her peers. Father is a Nurturer. Mother is a Jurist.
3. release; public apology
4. unsure; doesn't seem to be familiar

Chapter 2
1. rituals; Ceremonies in December as various childhood passages are celebrated
2. to follow the rules and use precise language
3. The children receive their assignments, their life's work.

Chapter 3
1. They are not forbidden but they are rarely used. Individualism is not a valued item.
2. Birthing and nurturing are separated. Birthing is not highly prized and honored.
3. Its appearance changes as Jonas looks at it. He wants to figure it out.

Chapter 4
1. The volunteer experiences have shown them a natural inclination for their assignments. Jonas does not show such a clear direction.
2. It is OK to see the old undressed so he feels less concern following the prohibition against seeing another undressed.
3. It's a matter of concern and shame for all but the old for whom it follows a celebration of their life.
4. mirth; such committees are very slow, rarely reaching any conclusion at all

Chapter 5
1. Sexual urges are suppressed with medication.
2. for emphasis

Chapter 6
1. excitement for most, apprehension for twelves
2. Considerable; They seem to make all decisions of importance.

© Novel Units, Inc. All rights reserved

Chapter 7
1. At the start he is expectant, apprehensive, uncertain because none of the assignments described by the Chief Elder seem to fit for him. He is even more apprehensive when his number (19) is skipped.
2. Answers vary.
3. The Elders observe the children and generally seem to make good choices of assignments, as well as they could observe. Some talent that isn't observable might be missed.

Chapter 8
1. He will be the Receiver of Memories. *Select* means to choose in preference to others, to pick out. *Assign* means to appoint, designate, name. The Chief Elder, being aware of clarity of language, would understand the difference in terms.
2. The term isn't specifically defined in this chapter. It seems to deal with how Jonas sees things, his perception.
3. This selection is an honor and he will fill a very important post.

Chapter 9
1. Jonas' friends are more in awe of him; he is no longer one of the gang.
2. The instructions are in opposition to many of the rules he'd learned in childhood.
3. Answers will vary. Some of the instructions are in contrast to usual expected behavior.

Chapter 10
1. He will somehow receive memories from The Giver who places his hands on Jonas' bare back.
2. snow
3. Several unusual things have happened—the instructions, the Old Receiver's house, and being able to turn off the speaker.

Chapter 11
1. like an expansion of his consciousness, not particularly dramatic to start and not very painful
2. The society apparently chose sameness to control dangers and to increase efficiency.
3. He calls out "Ouch" loudly.

Chapter 12
1. He is beginning to see the color red.
2. One-generation memories are memories of one's own personal experiences. The memory Jonas is receiving is of the corporate experiences of the world, a kind of history.

Chapter 13
1. As his consciousness/seeing beyond is expanded, he grows to appreciate color and other pleasantnesses. He figures that these experiences and awarenesses would be pleasant for everyone.
2. Answers vary; they may include, as plusses, efficiency, freedom from dangers, predictability and sameness. Minuses include the society being boring, unexciting, and uncreative.

Chapter 14
1. He aches and hurts and asks for relief-of-pain.
2. They don't have the same level of sensory awareness and so don't have the capacity to understand what's happening to Jonas in his training.
3. He is uncertain about how The Giver would react to his giving a pleasant memory to Gabriel.

Chapter 15
1. Jonas takes some of The Giver's pain.
2. war

Chapter 16
1. He is receiving more and more painful memories. The honor and wisdom of the position isn't enough for the pain.
2. His society doesn't teach those values.
3. Jonas has learned a deeper more intense meaning of love and caring. His parents respect and appreciate other people.

Chapter 17
1. The parents conduct a predictable, caring orderly life with few deep feelings. Jonas is learning of intense emotions.
2. innocence; an orderly, predictable life

Chapter 18
1. the Receiver-in-training who failed and requested release after five weeks of training
2. The Receiver holds all the memories of past lives and experiences for the whole community.

Chapter 19
1. To emphasize the question. In this instance The Giver is giving Jonas the choice. Jonas hesitates, is supported and pushed by The Giver, and then decides to see the morning's release. Jonas gains increased understanding and horror of his society.
2. Jonas learns that release is killing. He feels a terrible pain.

Chapter 20
1. The Giver explains that the book's society has systematically removed choice and deep emotions and real feeling. They don't have Jonas' depth of understanding. They can't (and don't) make moral decisions.
2. He is the only one in the society with the memories and with the depth of understanding.
3. Jonas will escape to Elsewhere. The memories he has received will be let loose in the society. The citizens will be forced to feel and cope with increased awareness.

Chapter 21
1. No; Gabriel is set for release so Jonas runs away earlier than planned. He takes his father's bicycle, rides at night, and hides during the day.

Chapter 22
1. landscape variations, trees, hunger, birds, wildflowers, hills
2. He wants only to save Gabriel.

Chapter 23
1. weather - extremes of cold threaten Jonas and Gabriel's survival
   snow - amount of snow make progress on the bicycle impossible
   sled - means for them to travel down the hill and out of the danger of the weather to another society
   music - what Jonas heard at the end of the book - suggests survival and hope at the end

Comprehension Check #1
Part I

1– D.   6– F.
2– J.   7– E.
3– M.   8– A.
4– H.   9– G.
5– B.   10– C.

Part II
Answers will vary. Students might trade their word maps for checking.

Part III
Use the rubric to analyze. Count up the number of points each student makes in the description. Look for at least five details.

Comprehension Check #2
Part I
Use the rubric. Count up details in the drawings. Look for at least ten details.

Part II
Suggested answers; accept any reasonable alternatives.

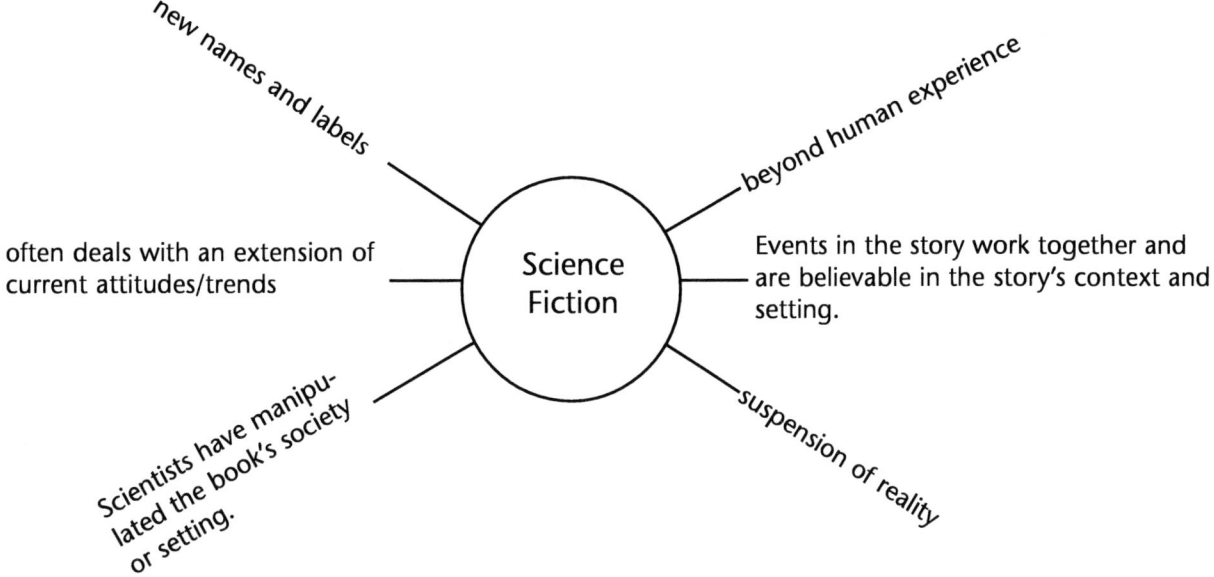

Comprehension Check #3
1. Use the rubric to analyze. Expect a coherent paragraph with at least three changes in Jonas.
2. Suggested answers only

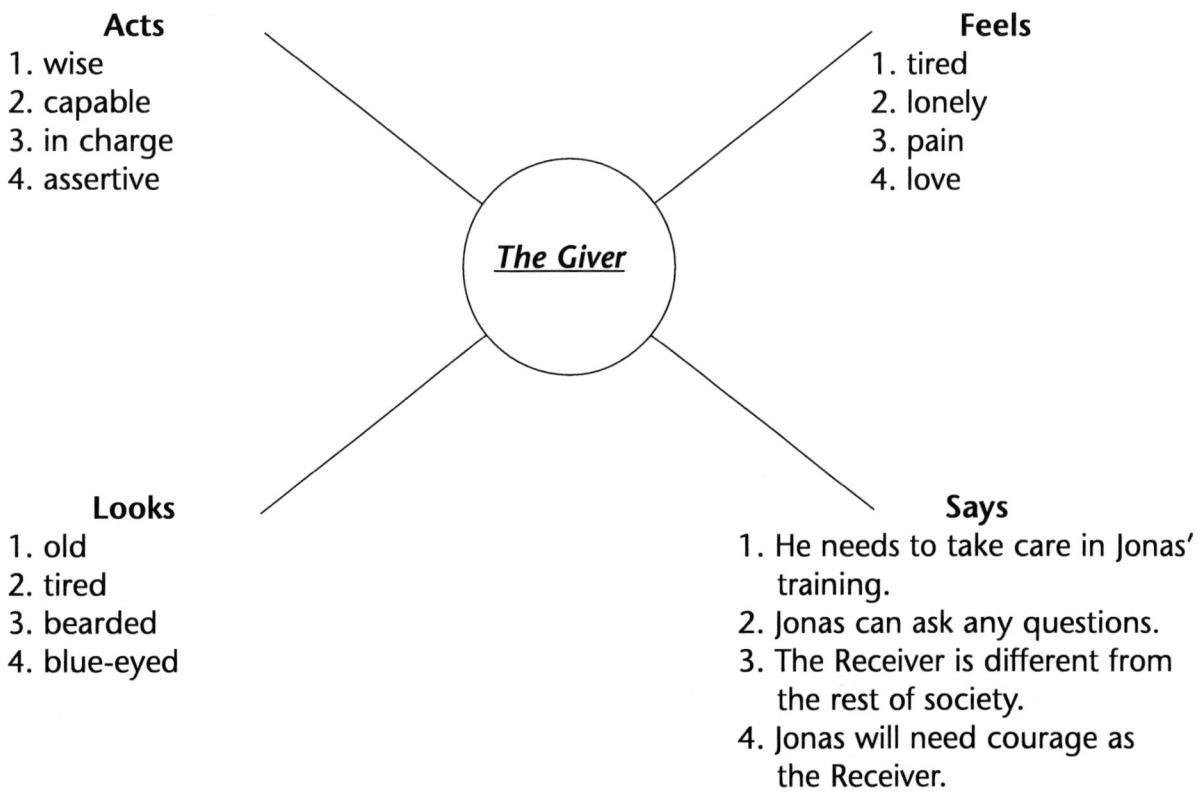

Naming

1. E
2. H.
3. F.
4. G. (page 11)
5. B. (page 16)
6. I. (page 102)
7. A.
8. J.
9. C.
10. D. (page 158)

The Great Prefix and Suffix Search

–ful	full of
–ous	characterized by
in–	not
inter–	between
ex–	out of
trans–	across/beyond
non–	not
dis–	not

Number Brain Teasers for Fun

26 letters in the alphabet
7 days of the week
13 in a bakers dozen
50 states in the union
52 cards in a deck
10 years in a decade
88 piano keys
24 hours in a day
9 justices in the Supreme Court
8 sides on a stop sign
5 digits in a zip code

Final Examination Answers

Part I

1– I.	6– L.	11– G.
2– O.	7– H.	12– C.
3– M.	8– E.	13– D.
4– J.	9– N.	14– F.
5– B.	10– A.	15– K.

Part II

1– D.	6– E.
2– G.	7– F.
3– I.	8– A.
4– C.	9– B.
5– J.	10– H.

Part III—See the Rubric

A. Following are the significant events/stages to be included.
   - Birth–Birthing Mother
   - Nurturing Center
   - Assignment to a Family Unit + Naming + Numbering
   - Education
   - Ceremony of Twelve– Assignment of Life's work
   - Establish own Family Unit
   - House of the Old

B. See the rubric. Look for clear expression as well as accurate depiction and book support for ideas expressed.

C. Ideas must be supported. Themes could include order vs chaos, efficiency vs randomness. The author affirms creativity and feelings and emotions as essential to the quality human experience.

D. See the rubric. Look for clear expression as well as accurate supported ideas.

Essay Evaluation Form

1.	**Focus:** Student writes a clear thesis and includes it in the opening paragraph.	10	8	4
2.	**Organization:** The final draft reflects the assigned outline; transitions are used to link ideas.	20	16	12
3.	**Support:** Adequate quotes are provided and are properly documented.	12	10	7
4.	**Detail:** Each quote is explained (as if the teacher had not read the book); ideas are not redundant.	12	10	7
5.	**Mechanics:** Spelling, capitalization, and usage are correct.	16	12	8
6.	**Sentence Structure:** The student avoids run-ons and sentence fragments.	10	8	4
7.	**Verb:** All verbs are in the correct tense; sections in which plot is summarized are in the present tense.	10	8	4
8.	Total effect of the essay.	10	8	4
		100	80	50

Comments:

Total:_____

(This rubric may be altered to fit the needs of a particular class. You may wish to show it to students before they write their essays. They can use it as a self-evaluation tool, and they will be aware of exactly how their essays will be graded.)

© Novel Units, Inc.   All rights reserved